Susan Olsen Stevens

The Little Golden Book of Metacognition

Susan Olsen Stevens

Dr. Goodreader Publishing

Crescent Beach, Florida

ISBN-13: 978-1973714712

ISBN-10: 197371471X

Cognitive learning. | Metacognition learning. | Education, Pre-school. |
Education, Elementary. | Education, Secondary

Printed and bound in the United States by CreateSpace

Dedicated to the team of friends and family who totally pretended that my constant talk about metacognition and growth mindset wasn't driving them a little bit nuts. You know who you are.

CONTENTS

INTRODUCTION

> Proficient readers, sometimes automatically, sometimes purposefully, must first be meta-cognitive: they must be aware of their own comprehension.
>
> If we know that thinking about our own thinking and using the strategies that form this metacognitive foundation are associated with the tendency to read more deeply, critically, analytically, and independently, shouldn't comprehension strategy instruction be a major focus of our work with children who are learning to read and reading to learn?
> - Elin Keene and Susan Zimmermann *Mosaic of Thought*

I wrote my first book, *Dr. Goodreader*, in 2012 which launched my journey into metacognition. That opening chapter serves as a fine introduction to this book:

"When [my co-planner, Rakitia, and I] began the self-monitoring unit, we set our over-arching goal: The students will use metacognition (thinking about their thinking) when they read.

This includes:

- Knowing when you know,
- Knowing when you don't know,
- Thinking about your own thinking,
- Knowing what you need to know when you're reading, and
- Knowing how to solve problems when meaning breaks down.

Whew! What a mouthful! We realized many of our students blithely kept on reading when they hadn't understood anything for pages and pages. We also soon realized that our lowest readers had a common characteristic – they didn't make a movie in their minds when they read. Another challenge we faced was that many students and their parents thought the ability to decode words and read quickly meant the children were good readers. They left comprehension out of the picture. We needed to rise to the challenge of not only educating the students but of educating their parents as well.

For example, many think that a good reader is a fast reader. That may be

true in some cases, but recent research shows that this is not guaranteed.
> Walczyk and Griffith-Ross (2007) report that 'slowing down' is the most commonly used strategy when readers encounter difficulty. The second strategy is rereading. Both result in better comprehension. Pressley found that 'children can often read with great speed and accuracy and yet recall few of the ideas in the text they read.' (2006, 209). In a similar vein, Buly and Valencia found that nearly 20% of their struggling readers could read fast and accurately but exhibit almost no recall or understanding of what they could read. While focusing instruction on reading faster may generate observed gains on rate/fluency measures, such gains do not indicate that children are improving as readers. – Bess Altwerger, Nancy Jordan, and Nancy Rankie Sheton Rereading Fluency – Process, Practice and Policy, Heinemann 2007, p. vii.

Interesting, eh? To begin with, Rakitia [my co-planner] and I talked through beliefs that were important to us. We didn't list them in an organized fashion, but they were part of our discussions always:

- We need to develop ways to explicitly teach each point. Anything that is learned must be explicitly taught.

- We need to communicate a sense of importance and urgency with each lesson.

- We need to model EVERYTHING.

- We need to grapple with how best to gradually release control into the hands of the students.

- We need to face the challenge of teaching the students to be active and not passive readers

- We need to serve as coaches who help our students develop their reading muscles.

- We need to think metacognitively about our own reading to better teach metacognition to our students.

(Teacher beware: As you consciously begin to think this way while you read, it may affect your brain strangely for a while. We've found that we are so focused on the strategies that our brains tend to be obsessively metacognitive when we read.)"[1]

You this read wrong.

I hope you just experienced a metacognitive shift. You read it, understood it, puzzled over it, went back and checked—and all in a millisecond. Not all problems are so easy to solve, which is why we need to teach metacognitive skills to our students.

> Metacognition is "thinking about thinking to improve learning."

My working definition for metacognition is "thinking about thinking to improve learning." However, I think we can benefit from a complete definition:

> Metacognition refers to awareness of one's own knowledge—what one does and doesn't know—and one's ability to understand, control, and manipulate one's cognitive processes (Meichenbaum, 1985).

It includes knowing when and where to use particular strategies for learning and problem solving as well as how and why to use specific strategies.

Metacognition is the ability to use prior knowledge to plan a strategy for approaching a learning task, take necessary steps to problem solve, reflect on, and evaluate results, and modify one's approach as needed (Teal, 2012)[1]

Metacognition has two main categories: Metacognitive Knowledge and Metacognitive Regulation.

Metacognitive Knowledge is knowing what you know and what you don't know. Sometimes we need to calibrate metacognitive knowledge due to a metacognitive misconception. For example, I had a group of 6th-grade students who way overvalued their ability to write. I researched and found that they had been receiving A's in elementary school for work, that to me, was just passable.

So, I taught them the 6-Traits and had them score a piece of writing. After they scored the writing, I showed them the official scores. They were stunned, and could finally see the metacognitive miscalculation they held about their own writing. I had another student who believed when writing a summary that longer was better. His fluid, but lengthy style had been rewarded in elementary school. It wasn't until he received pithy guidelines for writing summaries and the assurance that more was not better, that he changed his misconception.

Metacognitive Knowledge also includes knowing about **person, task, and strategy variables.** I believe the more we teach this, the better. When I worked at Country Day School in Costa Rica, the middle school began the year with Boot Camp. During Boot Camp, each discipline was assigned certain skills to teach. English Language Arts teachers might teach note-taking skills to be used in all subjects and do close readings of the school mission and vision statements. Social Studies teachers might have students take personality type, learning style, and multiple intelligence quizzes and explain the results to the students. Other disciplines had other tasks to accomplish. Although teachers complained about the time initially, we saw the benefit to the students at the end.

Each of these questions could easily become a mini-lesson or a part of an unofficial Boot Camp for your students.

Metacognitive Regulation is seldom taught and always needed. It includes planning, monitoring, evaluating, reflecting, and revising. As with the metacognitive knowledge cards, each of the metacognitive regulation cards could become a mini-lesson.

Plan	Monitor	Evaluate	Reflect
How will I approach this task?	Does this make sense?	Do I need to check my metacognitive calibration?	Create: What should I do next?
How much effort will this take?	Am I doing my best work? Am I in an optimal environment?	What works and what could I improve?	Evaluate: How well have I done?
How much memory will this take?	Does this feel familiar, difficult? Do I feel confident or uncertain?	What would I do differently next time?	Analysis: Do I see any patterns in what I've done?
How should I allocate my time?	Am I focused? Do I need a break? Sleep?	How can I scaffold this task to begin work again?	Apply: Where can I use this again?
Am I working alone or with others?	How is this working?	Am I finished?	Understand: What was important?
			Remember: What did I do?

I used to look at metacognition as the same thing as self-monitoring and you can see here that self-monitoring is a small, but key part of metacognition. Let me give you an example of metacognitive regulation gone awry in my life a few weeks ago.

Our condo is tiled in Mexican Saltillo tiles. Guests were coming and I really wanted things to look great and the tile grout was a little stained in a few places in the kitchen. Being a Pinterest addict, I checked for a solution. White vinegar and baking soda will do the trick, I read. Did I read the directions? No. I just got down on my hands and knees and began to shake out baking soda into a small area and then pour vinegar on top. It was fun- -like making volcanic eruptions in 3rd grade. I continued through the kitchen on my hands and knees with a scrub brush and when I stood up I had my first tinglings of misgiving. Would I be able to get it off? I washed it six times with clean water and a sponge mop and my son washed it twice with a mop before we got most of it off. The next day I washed it two more times with water and a little soap and it was finally presentable—BUT THE GROUT STAINS HADN'T DISAPPEARED. I did a lousy job with planning and monitoring, but did a great job with evaluation: Try cleaning materials out on a small area next time.

There is one more step under metacognitive regulation and that is Revise.

As a teacher, one of the questions I most hated was, "Is this good enough?" "Good enough for what?" I usually answered. At the same time, we can't keep revising forever and we must come to a point when we decide we've done the best we can in the time allotted.

Revise

How can I use what I have discovered to make this better?

Here is a simplified form of the metacognition regulation matrix. As you can see it is recursive and not linear. We plan and then evaluate our plan. Then we may revise the plan, re-evaluate, and move into the monitoring phase.

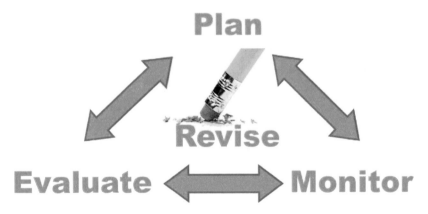

What Metacognition Overlaps It's difficult to think of all the pieces of what we are supposed to be teaching above and beyond content. One thing that causes me to breathe a sigh of relief is the incredible overlap metacognition has with many of these areas. Take a look at this Emotional Intelligence diagram and you can quickly see how Self-Awareness and Self-Management link to Person and Strategy Variables, Planning, and Monitoring.

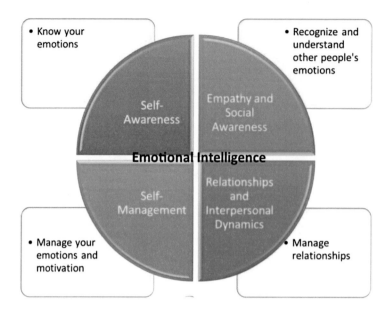

There is also a close connection to the **Four C's of 21st Century Skills**. When creating, one must use all the metacognitive skills. When collaborating you use many of the skills plus build our metacognitive skills as we learn from others. The old "two minds are better than one." We should also use metacognition in critical thinking and thoughtful communicating!

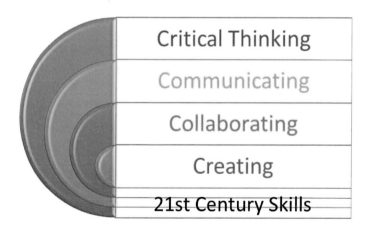

As you can see in this **Critical Thinking** diagram, metacognition is present here as well. I would say that at least in evaluating and analyzing major amounts of metacognitive skills are used and all of the critical thinking skills should use the plan – monitor – evaluate portions of metacognition.

Problem Solving is another area that overlaps with metacognition. When Identifying and Defining the Problem you need to look at task variables; when Exploring the Problem, you need to look at strategy variables, person variables, metaknowledge, and meta-comprehension. When Taking Action you need to plan, monitor, and evaluate. When Looking Back you are evaluating and reflecting.

Executive Functions is another area where we see tons of overlap:

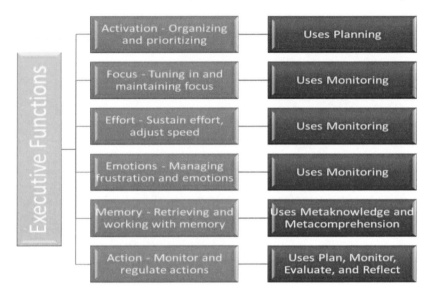

Inquiry is another exciting educational movement that overlaps with metacognition. Inquiry and metacognition are linked in many scholarly papers.

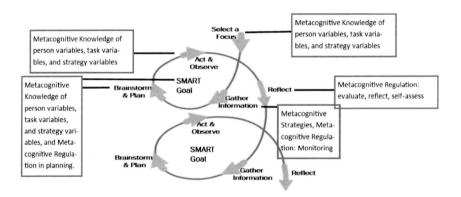

The last overlap we're going to look at is **Fixed/Growth Mindset.** Your mindset will affect every area of metacognitive thinking and in order to use growth mindset, you need to use ALL of the metacognitive areas. We will look at Growth/Fixed Mindset more thoroughly in Chapter 5.

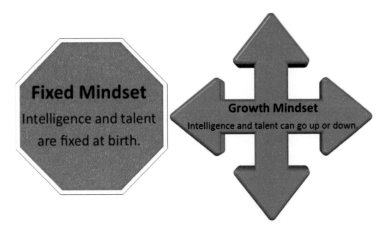

If we take time teaching metacognition, we have at least begun to teach a lot of the overlapping areas. The overlap ends up being a time saver and can even be built upon from grade level to grade level.

2. WHY TEACH METACOGNITION?

> Ultimately the potential benefit to the teacher of an embedded metacognitive approach is that there is a culture of learning, and talking about learning, in the classroom. This culture will support pupils to achieve their potential as learners and to tackle the new and the challenging. Furthermore, it will help students to have a secure understanding of the many ways in which they learn, and how they might learn even better.
>
> *-Metacognition in the Primary Classroom* by Tarrant and Holt

A lot of research has been done about the benefits of teaching metacognition, I'm happy to say.

- In a meta-analysis of 91 studies, Wang, Haertal, and Walberg (1993) determined that metacognition is the **number one shared characteristic of high academic achievers.**[1]

- Research supports the importance of metacognition for **learning across contexts** and provides a wide body of evidence **that metacognitive strategies can be taught and learned** (Bransford, Brown, & Cocking, 2000; Efklides & Misailidi, 2010; Hacker, Dunlosky, & Graesser, 2009; Hartman, 2002; Lai, 2011; Winne & Azevado, 2014.[2]

- In fact, students as young as 3 can be taught to use metacognition (Wilson & Conyers, 2016; Fisher, Frey & Hattie, 2016).

- A 2014 study by Veenman and colleagues suggests that the ability to apply a **metacognitive approach to learning may account for some 40 percent of the variation** in academic achievement across a range of outcomes (Wilson & Conyers, 2016).[4]

- **Metacognition is ranked 14th in 150 educational influences** on student learning by John Hattie's visible learning meta-analyses of "1,200 meta-analyses, with over 70,000 studies and 300 million students."[5]

- **Skilled comprehenders use metacognitive strategies significantly more often than less skilled readers**. Less skilled comprehenders were significantly less likely to make inferences from text <u>even with the equal background knowledge</u>...[emphasis added] This supports the notion that comprehension requires flexible simultaneous consideration of multiple elements. The extent to which children slow down their reading on encountering inconsistent information is a significant predictor of comprehension.[6]

- Transfer can be improved by helping students become more aware of themselves as learners who actively monitor their learning strategies and resources and assess their readiness for particular tests and performances. **Metacognitive approaches to instruction have been shown to increase the degree to which students will transfer to new situations** without the need for explicit prompting.

  o Teaching practices **congruent with a metacognitive approach to learning include those that focus on sense-making, self-assessment, and reflection** on what worked and what needs improving. These practices have been shown to increase the degree to which students transfer their learning to new settings and events.

  o **Because metacognition often takes the form of an internal dialogue, many students may be unaware of its importance unless the processes are explicitly emphasized by teachers.** Research has demonstrated that children can be taught these strategies, including the ability to predict outcomes, explain to oneself, note failures to understand, activate background knowledge, plan, and apportion time and memory...[7]

- Research by the Sutton Trust in the Education Endowment Foundation Toolkit rates metacognitive skills as one of the cheapest interventions schools can do, with learners making an **average of 8 months additional progress**. This is because it doesn't require expensive materials and the impact can be so large. These findings have shown that **metacognitive skills and metacognitive strategies are especially effective for pupil premium students** [schools that receive extra funding for disadvantaged students in the UK].[8]

- Metacognition leads to **active, not passive learning**. "Knowledge is considered to be metacognitive if it is actively used in a strategic manner to ensure that a goal is met. For example, a student may use knowledge in planning how to approach a math exam: "I know that I (person variable) have difficulty with word problems (task variable), so I will answer the computational problems first and save the word problems for last (strategy variable)." Simply possessing knowledge about one's cognitive strengths or weaknesses and the nature of the task without actively utilizing this information to oversee learning is not metacognitive."[9]

- At a recent international workshop, philosophers and neuroscientists gathered to discuss self-awareness and how it is linked to metacognition. Scientists believe that self-awareness, associated with the paralimbic network of the brain, serves as a "tool for monitoring and controlling our behavior and adjusting our beliefs of the world, not only within ourselves but, importantly, between individuals." **This higher-order thinking strategy actually changes the structure of the brain, making it more flexible and open to even greater learning.**[10]

- **Metacognition lies at the heart of all learning:** "the ultimate outcome of the journey [from brain toward mind] is to understand your own understanding" (Zull, 2011, p. 15).[11]

- **Deep learning promotes metacognition strategies**, strategic thinking, critical thinking, reasoning skills, connections to relevant learning, and creativity. Thus, students are able to integrate information learned in order to enhance integrative learning experiences.[12] [I would be willing to say that the reverse is also true: meta-cognitive strategies promote deep learning.]

- ". . . teaching students how to learn is as important as teaching them content because acquiring both the right learning strategies and background knowledge is important—if not essential—for **promoting lifelong learning**."[13]

- "Perhaps the most important reason for developing metacognition is that it can improve the application of **knowledge, skills**, and **character qualities** in realms beyond the immediate context in which they were learned."[14]

Every teacher I know desires to have a classroom with a thinking climate. However, this desire can be quenched by the many stresses involved in day to day teaching: assessment, coverage, a plethora of standards to teach, not to mention classroom management and interruptions of the teaching day.

"Metacognitive strategies instruction is still not commonly observed in most primary and secondary classrooms, and interviews with teachers have revealed limited knowledge about metacognition and how to foster it."[15]

Let's take a look at the two biggest reasons people give not to teach metacognitively.

3. MORE MONEY, MORE TIME? FROM WHERE?

> The most effective method of ensuring more engagement is not through any particular strategy, but through a more radical rethinking of time. When we think in terms of students' engagement, the question of allocating time shifts from "How do I as a teacher choose to use my allotted class time to accomplish my goals?" to "How will I enable my students to use their time in class to maximize their learning?"
>
> --*Creating Cultures of Thinking* by Ron Ritchhart

The first objection to teaching metacognitively is **"Where will we get the money for yet another school program?"**

In this visual put out by the Education Endowment Foundation Toolkit, we see the effectiveness of educational influences combined with their cost. Items higher on the graph are more effective than items lower on the graph. Items on the left of the graph cost less than items on the right of the graph.

Toolkit findings

16

Yes, teaching metacognitively does take a little money—for training or books—but you don't need a program to be effective. What you do need is buy-in by a few teachers who are willing to be turn-key teachers—to turn around and teach what they have learned to other teachers. Metacognition can also be instituted as a trickle-up strategy by a passionate teacher or two who want to create an energizing thinking environment in their classrooms.

When I taught at InterAmerican Academy in Guayaquil, Ecuador we were required to visit other classrooms once a quarter. We began by randomly choosing who we wanted to visit and later asked teachers to choose to visit classrooms to learn about a school initiative. For example, when we were adding reading and writing workshop to the school PK – 8th grade, teachers would sign up for demo lessons on these topics. Sometimes the observations would be structured in such a way that observing teachers joined small groups and helped facilitate the work. These observations got everyone talking and learning and created communities of teaching.

We did something similar at Country Day School in Escazu, Costa Rica. Teachers were required to put a strength of theirs on a board such as "Active Learning in Math" or "Classroom Management," and all teachers were required to visit at least two classrooms that had a strength in which they wanted to improve.

I never in my life saw anything improve school morale in the way that happened when classroom peer visits were established at those two schools. People began sharing transparently about their practice and weaknesses and strengths. Teachers' meetings were energized as teachers shared what they'd learned.

I propose something similar when instituting metacognitive teaching. Teachers could sign up in pairs or as grade level teams, or any small group to observe each other on a steady basis throughout the school year with the idea of improving metacognitive practices in the classroom. Perhaps a minimum amount of visits could be specified with the understanding that we are trying to change practice at a foundational level and the more practice we get the better.

At both schools where we did this, teachers generally did the observations during a planning period, although if there was someone they really wanted to see teach at a particular time we would arrange for coverage for the class. This can be done efficiently by hiring a substitute teacher for a day or two and have teachers sign up for coverage hours on a schedule for observations.

The second question I often hear is, **"Where do I find the time?"** Anyone who has spent a few years in the classroom knows that this is a legitimate question—there never is enough time. And a teacher will fight the perception of time being taken away like a mother bear protecting her cubs. We even have a miserly way of speaking about time in English—how we spend it. In other languages, people pass the time, but we hoard it and spend it.

Experienced teachers know there are certain ways that we invest time that are time savers in the long run:

- Establishing classroom routines;
- Establishing classroom community;
- Doing class read-alouds;
- Creating and implementing class norms;
- Teaching discussion skills.

I believe that teaching cognitive strategies and metacognitive thinking is one of those investments that pays huge dividends in the end. I have a suggestion for how to achieve this in your classroom. For many years I've been using Steven Covey's Organizational Matrix in my life. The general idea goes like this:

MANAGE	FOCUS
Crises & Pressing Problems	On Strategies & Values
Demand & Necessity Daily Crises Be Quick to Delegate	Planning for Learning Keep Critical Thinking Consider the Big Picture
IMPORTANT AND URGENT	**IMPORTANT NOT URGENT**
AVOID	LIMIT
Interruptions & Busy Work	The Trivial & Wasteful
Illusion & Deception Not Your Emergency Minimize Investment	Escape & Waste Entertainment Only Used to Minimize Stress
URGENT NOT IMPORTANT	**NOT IMPORTANT OR URGENT**

In life, we tend to spend time in quadrants 1,3, and 4. Covey's idea is that we plan to spend time in quadrant 2. I challenge you to use Covey's Matrix to set your priorities for the school year. Here are some ideas to get you thinking:

MANAGE	FOCUS
Crises & Pressing Problems	On Strategies & Values
Standard Coverage Lock down drills Student is sick Prepare for state exams	Exercise Explicit lessons in metacognitive and cognitive strategies. Read alouds Independent Reading
IMPORTANT AND URGENT	**IMPORTANT NOT URGENT**
AVOID	**LIMIT**
Interruptions & Busy Work	The Trivial & Wasteful
Interruptions for bathroom, etc. (avoid by having systems in place) Grading worksheets	Transition time Coloring (books) Letter soups Worksheets
URGENT NOT IMPORTANT	**NOT IMPORTANT OR URGENT**

And after we set our priorities, we need to plan for our priorities. If we start from our priorities and not from the mindset of, "How am I going to shoehorn one more thing into my day?" we can make it happen.

Another way to structure your thinking about time is to create a mission question that you refer to when making any decision about learning. Some examples might be:

- Am I planning for student thinking?
- Is everything I'm doing today helping students learn how to learn?
- Am I giving students the tools they need to learn metacognitively and independently?

19

- Are my students thinking about their thinking today?

I prefer mission questions to mission statements because a question forces us to continually examine what we are doing. I got this idea from *A More Beautiful Question: The Power of Inquiry to Spark Breakthrough Ideas* by Warren Berger.

Time is a precious commodity, let's make sure we're spending/using/passing it in a way that is best for our students' learning and in the long run, good for us. After all, what do we treasure more as teachers but those moments in our teaching lives where real engaged thinking and learning are happening?

4. COGNITIVE ASSET TOOLS

> When you decrease your focus on what is wrong (**deficit-based thinking**) and increase your focus on what is right (**Asset-Based Thinking**), you build enthusiasm and energy, strengthen relationships, and move people and productivity to the next level.
>
> *--Change the Way You See Everything through Asset-Based Thinking* by Dathryn Cramer and Hank Wasiak

I have trained many teachers how to confer in reading and writing workshop. The most difficult parts of this training is moving teachers from deficit-based conferring to asset-based conferring. In writing, many teachers only felt comfortable correcting something that was wrong with the writing—and generally only at the conventions level. They would point out that the student had made spelling mistakes and tell them how to correct them. Or they would correct a decoding mistake in reading without any teaching about how to avoid the mistake in the future. Their time would be better used to point out assets. "You really chose a powerful verb there, do you think there's anywhere else that could use a powerful verb?" "You sounded just like you talk when you wrote this. Great voice!"

In my personal life, there are times when I can only see my husband's faults—another example of deficit thinking. I call it The Devil's Magnifying Glass. Whether in school or at home we need to get out of the habit of deficit thinking. Let's look at the cognitive assets that are necessary for metacognition:

- Maintain an outlook of practical optimism about their learning performance,
- Set learning goals and plan to achieve them,
- Focus their selective attention and optimize working memory,
- Monitor their learning progress, and
- Apply their learning experiences across core subjects and in their personal lives.[1]

According to Wilson and Conyers, all of these assets can be taught, but the first one, the practical optimism or "Can or Can't Do" attitude is also inherited. Interesting. We can inherit practical optimism or practical pessimism. So, we may have some extra work with the first asset—as we work to undo an "I Can't" attitude. We'll look at this in the next chapter.

When we're looking for cognitive assets we need to know what they are in order to identify them in our students. Here's a three-part list adapted from Mel Levine's *Concentration Cockpit* as well as Wilson and Conyers *Teaching Students How to Drive Their Brains*:

Input Phase	Processing Phase	Output Phase
Metacognition	Define the problem	Audience
Clear intent	Classify	Thoughtful
Practical optimism	Make connections	Effective expression
Initiative	Plan	Courage/Risk taking
Systematic search	Cognitive Flexibility	Finishing power
Using two of more	Make inferences	Learn from experience
sources of information	Make meaning	Thinks ahead
Selective attention	Monitor understanding	Examines options
Make comparisons	Summarize	Paces appropriately
Understand time	Visualize	Realistic self-evaluation
Understand space	Troubleshoot	Collaborates
Persistence (Grit)	Evaluate	
Alertness	Mental effort	
Collaborates	Consistency	
	Stamina (Grit)	
	Collaborates	
Questions		
Have I gathered enough pertinent information? Have I focused my concentration on the task?	How is this information important to me? What is my plan for using this information?	Who is my audience? How can I best communicate this to my audience?

If we know cognitive assets and begin to look for and comment upon them, I believe we will see incredible growth in our classroom environment—both academically and in the whole child. Make it a point to celebrate these assets both privately and publicly.

5. MINDSETS

Research on **brain plasticity** has shown how connectivity between neurons can change with experience. With practice, neural networks grow new connections, strengthen existing ones, and build insulation that speeds transmission of impulses. These neuroscientific discoveries have shown us that we can increase our neural growth by the actions we take, such as using good strategies, asking questions, practicing, and following good nutrition and sleep habits.

--mindsetworks.com

I think it's easier to show you about fixed and growth mindsets than to tell you.

Fixed Mindset	Growth Mindset
1. I'm good at it or not.	1. I can learn anything I put my mind to.
2. When it's hard, I give up.	2. When it's hard, I keep going.
3. I like to do things that are easy for me.	3. I love to challenge myself.
4. I feel small when I fail.	4. When I fail, I learn.
5. I like people thinking I'm smart.	5. I like people thinking I'm a hard worker.
6. When others succeed, I'm threatened.	6. When others succeed, I'm inspired.
I Can't-itis	Grit

When I first learned about fixed and growth mindsets I thought that I had a growth mindset, but as I looked more carefully over time I realized that I had more of a mixed to fixed mindset. I had always thought of myself as an overachiever, which I think would indicate that I had achieved more than my talents and IQ had predicted and thus a fixed mindset. I did know the benefit of hard work in over-achieving and so in that way perhaps I had a growth mindset.

I know I demonstrated a fixed mindset when I snuck into my darkened 3rd-grade classroom during recess and looked up my IQ score in my teacher's drawer. I was ashamed, but something inside me just needed to know if I were smart or not!

I've always thought of myself in these ways: Good at reading, pretty good at writing, somewhat artistic, not a math person, and not athletic AT ALL! It never occurred to me that I was good at the things I'd put effort into and not so good at the things I hadn't put much effort into. I got through high school math by going in for help every day before school, but with my fixed mindset that I was terrible at math "just like my mother" I never got very far with it—I just did good enough to get by with a grade that wouldn't hurt my GPA too much.

Now that I've learned about brain plasticity, I am working at getting off my mindset seesaw and firmly into a growth mindset. There are some areas that I am still waffling about—like whether I can strengthen my logical thinking. It's difficult to combat mindset that is firmly entrenched. Mine currently looks like this:

My Official Mindset Seesaw

I learned to speak Spanish with a lot of effort.

I can learn to think logically and analyze if I work at it.

I love to be challenged.

I am not a math person.

Logical thinking is not my thing.

I am not athletic, but everyone in my husband's family is blessed with that gift.

Growth Mindset   Fixed Mindset

What does your mindset see-saw look like? And how is it affecting your teaching? What is your mindset about your students? Do you believe they all can learn? All of them? How about your relationships? Do you believe that someone can change? That you can change? That the relationship can change? Mindset is all pervasive and affects every area of our lives.

One thing that always bugged my siblings and me was that our mom saw us as people who hadn't changed since childhood. "You're such a chameleon, Susie," really bothered me when I had (finally) developed firm principles and a strong sense of who I am.

We can get caught up in a vicious cycle or a virtuous cycle with our mindsets. Both of them can become self-fulfilling prophecies. Some things aren't worth expending the effort to learn—I'm ready to live with the fact that I'm not athletic because the time expenditure wouldn't be worth it to me. I'd rather spend my time reading and writing and creating in various ways. I do want to expend the time to get my drawing skills back. I haven't picked up an art supply for 13 years even though art was my major in college. It's time to go back, redevelop brain pathways and improve my skills.

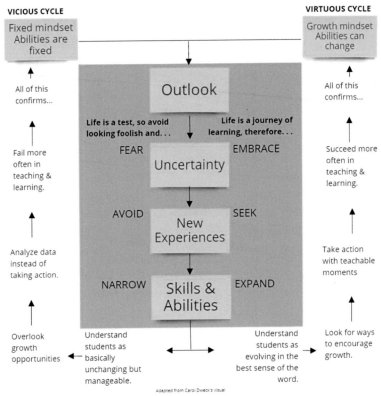

VICIOUS CYCLE		VIRTUOUS CYCLE

Adapted from Carol Dweck's visual

Another important aspect of Fixed and Growth Mindsets is the whole idea of what happens in our brains when we make a mistake. Here is what math guru, Jo Boaler, says about that in her amazing book, *Mathematical Mindsets*.

> Moser's study produced two important results. First, the researchers found that the students' brains reacted with greater ERN and Pe responses—electrical activity—when they made mistakes than when their answers were correct. Second, they found that the brain activity was greater following mistakes for individuals with a growth mindset than for individuals with a fixed mindset.
>
> The study also found that individuals with a growth mindset had a greater awareness of errors than individuals with a fixed mindset, so they were more likely to go back and correct errors.[1]

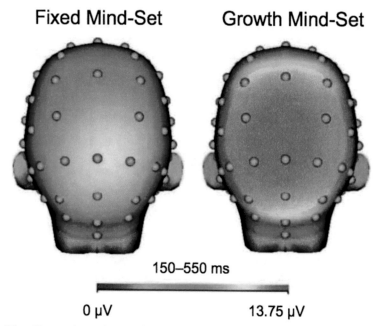

Fixed Mind-Set　　**Growth Mind-Set**

150–550 ms

0 µV　　　　　　　13.75 µV

The illustration above shows the amount of electrical activity that takes place in someone with a fixed mindset and someone with a growth mindset.[2]

Some of my favorite movies are based on a growth mindset: *Akeelah and the Bee, Freedom Writers, October Skies, Lean on Me, Stand and Deliver,* and *The Great Debaters* are just a few. Inspire yourself and your students with some of these gems.

6. METACOGNITION & LITERACY

In *Comprehension Connections: Bridges to Strategic Reading*,
Tanny McGregor devotes an entire chapter to metacognition,
explaining that she doesn't "know how to teach thinking strategies
unless [she begins] with metacognition.... In making kids aware of
how they think about their own thinking, [she opens] a channel
through which purposeful conversation can flow." McGregor
provides a "launching sequence" for metacognition that includes
concrete experiences, wordless picture books, a graphic organizer,
and easy-to-obtain tools (in this case, free paint chips from your
local home improvement store) to help students become
metacognitive about their reading. She also includes "thinking
stems," or sentence starters that can prompt reflective thinking
such as "I'm thinking..."; "I'm wondering..."; or "I'm noticing."

--http://beyondpenguins.ehe.osu.edu

Good readers know how to use cognitive and metacognitive
strategies together to develop a deeper understanding of a book's
theme or topic. They learn or "construct knowledge" (using
cognitive strategies) through a variety of methods, and then
recognize (using metacognitive strategies) when they lack
understanding and, consequently, choose the right tools to correct
the problem.

--http://www.benchmarkeducation.com

I didn't learn about reading strategies until I began teaching at Colegio
Americano in Quito, Ecuador in 1999. I'd always been a good reader and
loved reading and thought that once you learned to decode reading
comprehension came easily. Colegio Americano introduced me to many
reading/writing stars of the universe: Lucy Calkins, Irene Fountas and Gay
Su Pinnell, Jim Trelease, Nancy Atwell, Regie Routman, Harvey Daniels,

and Elin Oliver Keene, just to mention a few. Colegio Americano boasted a huge professional library and I (shamefacedly) admit that I had cheap copies of them made at the university for a dollar or two per book. (It is for this reason that I made my book, *Dr. Goodreader,* free to download from my website.) I spent six years digesting every word I could find on the topics of reading and writing. I saw reading strategies and the 6-traits of writing everywhere I looked. The reading and writing connection came alive to me. My life as a teacher and as a person was permanently changed.

And as I said, I began to see strategies everywhere. But when I taught the strategies my 5th-grade students didn't seem to know how or when to apply them in their reading. I sat down with my 3rd-grade teacher friend, Rakitia Delk, and we decided to create a flow chart that would help the students figure out when and how to use the strategies. Many planning periods, before school, and after school sessions later we unveiled Dr. Goodreader to our students.

Dressed up in doctor coats with stethoscopes around our necks, we told the children we were going to teach them how to be doctors—doctors of good reading who would learn how to diagnose and solve their own reading problems.

The thing is—it worked! We couldn't believe the difference it made. We created a lesson for each block and it gave the students a metacognitive framework of self-questioning to work with. You can download the chart on the next page and a blank one for students to fill out as you teach from my blog doctorgoodreader.edublogs.org.

It was kind of amazing—students began to metacognitively identify what was causing them problems in their reading. Students internalized Dr. G and by the time they were in middle school, all the teachers had to do was say, "What would Dr. Goodreader say?"

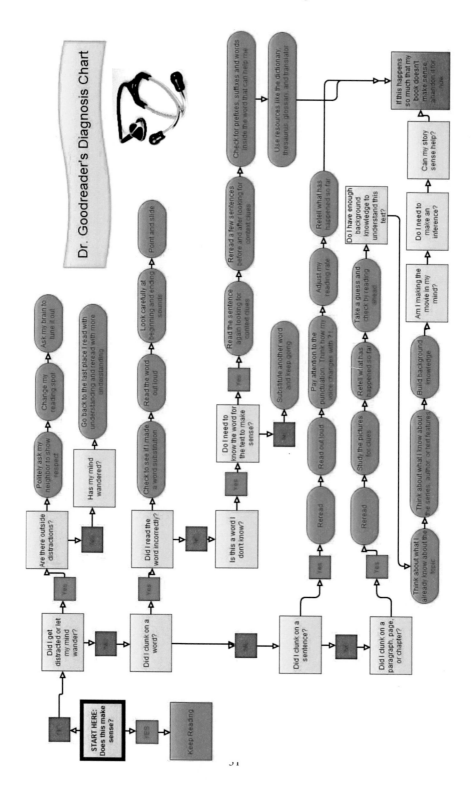

Dr. Goodreader's Diagnosis Chart

Of course, this isn't all you want to be working on in reading, and this reading pyramid gives an overview of what we want to be working on all the time. We don't have to wait to start developing the top areas of the pyramid with pre-reading students, we can work on them during read-alouds.

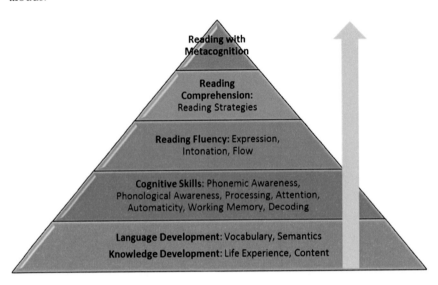

Another consideration for developing metacognition is Vygotsky's Zone of Proximal Development. Teaching in the ZPD maintains just enough challenge to push metacognitive thinking without frustration or boredom. We all know that it is difficult to maintain the ZPD in a classroom setting full of students with varied ZPDs, but it is easily achievable during reading and writing workshop—especially during conferring. My conferring bible is still Carl Anderson's *how's it going? A Practical Guide to Conferring with Student Writers*.

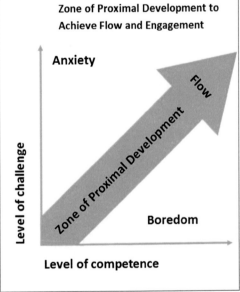

Part of teaching metacognitively is creating independent learners. The Gradual Release of

Ways of Assisting Readers Through Their Zones of Proximal Development: Modes of Scaffolding		
Teacher-Regulated	**Supportive Joint Practice**	**Student Regulated**
Teacher modeling Explicit instruction Reading to student	Independent Reading Reciprocal Reading Shared reading Small Group Inquiry Guided Reading Literature Circles	Independent Reading Students use strategy(ies) alone in context of Inquiry Project
Teacher chooses material for teaching purposes.	Reading material negotiated and matched to student needs.	Student chooses reading material.
I DO **YOU WATCH** _{Adapted from imaginetheirsiegroup.net}	**I DO** **YOU HELP** **YOU DO** **I HELP**	**YOU DO** **I WATCH**

Responsibility Framework gives teachers a way to help students grow to independence and gives us a way to use the Zone of Proximal Development at the classroom level.

If all of this food for thought seems overwhelming, look at it as a smorgasbord. I suggest starting with small helpings and then go back for more. Keep it manageable. Or, if you're more like me you can load up your plate sky high and go for broke.

7. HOW TO TEACH METACOGNITION

- **Be intentional about teaching metacognitive skills.** When designing your course, identify opportunities in which to incorporate strategies to teach metacognitive skills. For example, you might decide to build metacognitive strategies into an assignment, or around your midterms. Decide when to focus on self-regulation skills and when to focus on guiding students to think metacognitively about course content.
- **Be explicit when teaching metacognitive skills**. Talk about metacognitive skills with your students; define metacognition and explain why developing metacognitive skills is important during and after university. . . . In other words, don't assume that students will automatically see relationships that might be obvious to you.
- **Don't overdo it.** Pick your spots and let other opportunities go. Students would be overwhelmed if most or all of the following strategies were incorporated into one course.[1]

--University of Waterloo Center for Teaching Excellence

Be Intentional About Teaching Metacognitive Skills

The Sutton Foundation and the Educational Endowment Foundation in the UK has developed these thoughts for teachers to consider before implementing metacognitive strategies in your classroom:

"Teaching approaches which encourage learners to plan, monitor and evaluate their learning have very high potential, but require careful implementation.

1. Have you taught pupils explicit strategies on how to plan, monitor and evaluate specific aspects of their learning? Have you given them opportunities to use them with support and then independently?

2. Teaching how to plan: Have you asked pupils to identify the different ways that they could plan (general strategies) and then how best to approach a particular task (specific technique)?

3. Teaching how to monitor: Have you asked pupils to consider where the task might go wrong? Have you asked the pupils to identify the key steps for keeping the task on track?

4. Teaching how to evaluate: Have you asked pupils to consider how they would improve their approach to the task if they completed it again?"[3]

We need to plan to teach strategies in all of these areas. I used to teach various ways to plan for writing: Sketch Notes, Cornell Notes, Mind Maps, Outlines, Brainstorming, etc. and once the students had the exposure to many methods they could choose the one which worked best for them for the task at hand.

To teach metacognitively you need to be intentional. One way to be intentional is to look at a lesson or a unit that you already teach and determine what metacognitive skills your students will need to complete the lesson. To get you started, there is a list of metacognitive language in Appendix B.

The book, *Metacognition in the Primary Classroom* is full of practical ideas that will spark your thinking. For example, Guess My Rule shows how you can easily include metacognitive thinking in a common primary lesson.

First, determine your Metacognition Targets:

Metacognition Targets	
Looking (observing	Listening
Remembering	Thinking
Guessing, which at this stage might incorporate: • Trying out • Making connections • Having a go • Working it out	

Then determine the I Can statements for your lesson:

- I can think about how things are alike and different.
- I can listen to the ideas of others.
- I can use my thinking to guess the rule.

35

Finally, introduce the lesson using metacognitive language and continue to use it during the lesson:

Guess My Rule: to play we are going to need to look carefully, listen, and think.

Teacher has two hoops and a group of small objects (animals, people, vehicles) in a range of sizes and colors.

Teacher explains the game using the targeted language.

"I'm going to put the giraffe in the red hoop and the snake in the blue hoop. Can anyone guess my rule (for sorting)?"

This goes on until someone guesses the rule, at which time the teacher says, "Now you have to remember the rule. Look carefully and tell me where to put this next one.[2]

Be Explicit About Teaching Metacognitive Skills

Whether you want to strengthen your teaching of metacognitive skills or begin teaching metacognitively, the first step is to be metacognitive yourself. I have developed my metacognitive skills by signing up with companies who need guinea pigs to test websites. You voice your thoughts as you complete tasks on the website while your screen and voice are taped. It's great practice for voicing your thinking and you get paid for it.

> The absolute, very best method for teaching students how to think metacognitively is through modeling.

We, teachers, need to develop our metacognitive awareness. I sympathize with my grand-daughter who is so frustrated when asked to explain how she solved a math problem. "I don't know. I just did it," she says. She is at the first level of metacognitive development and needs to be taught how to move further along the continuum. Where are you on this continuum? If you are like me you are in different places depending upon the subject matter. It is easy for me to communicate my thinking in a reading think-aloud, but difficult for me to communicate what I think about a painting. Like anything else, it just takes awareness and practice.

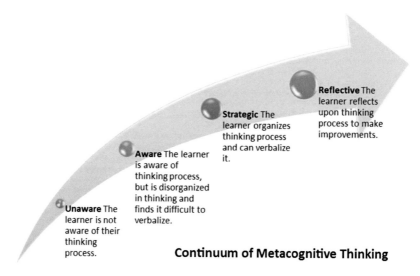

Reflective The learner reflects upon thinking process to make improvements.

Strategic The learner organizes thinking process and can verbalize it.

Aware The learner is aware of thinking process, but is disorganized in thinking and finds it difficult to verbalize.

Unaware The learner is not aware of their thinking process.

Continuum of Metacognitive Thinking

The absolute, very best method for teaching students how to think metacognitively is through modeling. We need to open up our brains to our students so they can see our thinking. When Rakitia and I developed Dr. Goodreader and began giving the lessons that went with it, EVERY time we had a lesson flop it was because we didn't take the time to model. EVERY TIME! If we think of our students as metacognitive apprentices, our role will shift a little bit from teaching to making the invisible visible to our students.

Think Aloud is a synonym for modeling. Here is what Jeffrey Wilhelm has to say about Think Alouds:

Think Alouds Can Target Common Troubles of Struggling Readers

- *Poor readers often plow right through a reading, decoding words but not comprehending the text.* Think alouds can help because they require the reader to slow down and to reflect on how they are understanding and interpreting text.

- *Poor readers don't bring meaning forward with them, building as they work through a text.* Think-alouds can help students to identify, consolidate, and summarize the growing meanings they make while reading so that the meaning can be used.

- *Poor readers just give up.* Think-alouds can help by giving students strategies to try in lieu of giving up. I'm indebted to the work of James Baumann and his colleagues in using think-alouds for monitoring comprehension. Their studies, among others, have shown that think alouds are a highly effective way to help students deal with the monitoring and repair of comprehension difficulties (See especially Baumann, 1986, 1992, 1993.)[4]

Think Alouds as Assessment We want to show our thinking to students, but we also want to help them to move up the metacognitive continuum and learn to communicate their thinking.

Students need to know the vocabulary of thinking to be able to do this. So first, introduce vocabulary little by little. *How to Teach Thinking Skills Within the Common Core* by Bellanca, Fogarty, and Pete is chock full of creative ideas for this.

Since less skillful readers have difficulty decoding and voicing their thinking at the same time, you can video the students while they read—perhaps during a DRA, and then show them the video right afterward and ask at key points, such as a self-correction, "What were you thinking then?"

And, of course, we need to be continually modeling this kind of behavior for students to be able to voice their thinking.

Getting Started With Metacognition

1. First, I would introduce the whole idea of **Fixed and Growth Mindset**. I might even have students take a little quiz to identify their mindsets before the teaching. I would explain the plasticity of the brain and let that vocabulary become part of my classroom.

2. Then with the focus on the brain, I would shift into **learning about themselves as learners** and how that knowledge can help us in practical ways.

   I remember having 5th – 7th-grade students take a multiple

intelligence test and we hung the results in the classroom. When the students formed small groups, I would tell them something like, "For this task you need to make sure you have a visual thinker, an interpersonal thinker, and a linguistic thinker in your group," which got them thinking about our different types of brains and different types of contributions we could make.

Another thing I've done along these lines is to have students take learning styles quizzes and then we would brainstorm ways that the types of learners would study for a test. I had one kinesthetic learner who was a competitive swimmer. He put the material he was studying on plasticized notecards at the end of his swimming lane and checked them every lap or two and thought about them as he swam.

3. After students learn about the brain and themselves, I would **teach them that they are in control of their brains** Using a lesson from *Teaching Students How to Drive Their Brains*. The metaphor they use about driving your brain is appealing to all ages—from young children pedaling around the playground to high school students about to get their licenses.

   The idea is to brainstorm with your students how road signs might correlate to our thinking and refer to them when working. For example:

| Am I distracted? | Stop and think about it. | Do I need to slow down? | Should I give someone else a chance to talk? |

4. As I mentioned in the last section, the students need to learn **cognitive/metacognitive vocabulary**. It is easy to assume that our students understand the vocabulary that we are using.

5. One of the most effective ways to have students work metacognitively is to collaborate. In collaborative groups with metacognitively structured activities, students can scaffold each others' thinking and gently push one another to think deeply. I

have no idea where I originally found this idea, just that it is not original, but one way to encourage good thinking in groups is to have Participation Quizzes where we assess what we value—great thinking and growth through collaboration.

First, you teach the **Participation Quiz** Goals and then you assess with anecdotal notes:

Participation Quiz Goals
During the participation quiz, I will be looking for: <ul><li>Listening to each other and giving equal air time,</li><li>Justifying thinking,</li><li>Making connections that help with understanding,</li><li>Explaining ideas clearly,</li><li>Asking clarifying questions,</li><li>Asking questions that deepen the discussion.</li></ul>
Participation Quiz Assessment

Group 1:	Group 2:	Group 3:
Quick start	Asking powerful	Totally off task
All working	questions	Redirected
together	Good group roles	Stayed off task
Deep discussion	"What do you	Given individual
"Let's go around	guys think?"	work
and see what	Good discussion	??
everyone things."	A	
A+		

6. I would teach **thinking routines**. Project Zero at Harvard University has developed Visible Thinking Routines for the general categories of understanding, fairness, truth, and creativity. The routines for the understanding module are:

- **What makes you say that?** A routine for looking closely, interpreting what is observed, and reasoning with evidence.
- **Think, Puzzle, Explore.** A routine for eliciting prior knowledge and developing curiosity about a topic.
- **Think, Pair, Share.** A routine for promoting communication and active engagement of all students.
- **Headlines.** A routine for summarizing and consolidating ideas, events, and experiences.
- **Question Starts.** A routine for activating curiosity and generating questions for exploration.
- **The Explanation Game.** A routine for building explanations about parts or features of something.
- **Connect, Extend, Challenge.** A routine for processing and making sense of new information.[5]

7. I would say the easiest way to begin having a more metacognitive classroom is to **ask probing questions**—specifically the type of questions that stimulate thinking about thinking and learning. However, when you begin asking these types of questions, students might begin playing the teacher guessing game. For example, if you ask, "Why did you choose that strategy?" the student might assume the strategy was incorrect and start guessing other strategies. We need to help our students become comfortable with questions.

What are you learning?
How are you learning?
Why did you choose that strategy?
How is that working for you?
Does that make sense?

What do you know about that?
What do you need to know about that?
How will you know when you've learned it?

What do you think?
Why do you think that?
How do you know that is true?
Can you tell me more?

What are you working on today in your reading/writing?
How's it going?
What would you like to do next?

8. I would institute some of the following **metacognitive practices**:
   - Self-assessments
   - Peer assessments like the Ladder of Feedback from Making Learning Visible:

- o Clarify – Ask genuine questions to understand.
- o Value – State what you value.
- o State concerns and make suggestions – "I wonder if…"
- Reflection time
- Traffic light cups (red, yellow, and green cups that students place on their desks to show level of understanding)
- Jig-Saw groups
- Exit tickets
- Reflection Manger group role
- Student-generated test questions
- Find your favorite mistake (look for conceptual mistakes)

In summary, here are some general tips for teaching metacognitive thinking:

- Understand **what children** bring to the table. (Know thy students.)
- Teach in **depth**, not an inch deep and a mile wide.
- **Integrate** metacognitive thinking in all subject areas.
- Do **think-alouds** and **model your thinking** including how you start, how you decide what to do next, how you check your work, and how you know when you are finished.
- Ask **probing questions.**
- **Focus on sense-making** and **reflection.**
- Have students **set learning goals, monitor progress,** and **self-assess.**

Don't Overdo It

At the end of my last coaching session with her, a high school teacher in New Jersey asked a great question: "Can you do too much metacognition teaching?" My answer was, "Absolutely!" and I went on to explain that we don't want to drive the students to boredom by repetition of the same strategy all the time—for example, I wouldn't put an exam wrapper on every exam. Nor would I ask why they chose a particular strategy in every conference.

Then I got to thinking about what a friend had explained to me about marketing and how important the role of repetition is. He talked about repetition fatigue and all sorts of interesting marketing concepts. Think of these slogans. Thanks to repetition marketing, most likely all of us can name the products being advertised here:

- **Got milk?**
- **Just do it.**
- **Plop, plop, fizz, fizz, oh what a relief it is.**

I think what I'm trying to say here, is that we need to walk a fine line between repetition fatigue (a.k.a. boredom and irritation) and familiarity. For example, I would repeat a thinking routine until the students were familiar and comfortable with it and then lengthen the time before I used it again. I would mix up the repertoire of metacognitive moves in my classroom. And I would keep my finger on both the pulse of the energy level in the classroom and of individual students—thinking metacognitively is draining, especially at first and we want our students to be challenged enough to be engaged, but not cognitively exhausted.

Metacognitive teaching is energizing as it encourages those moments we prize as educators—when real thinking and conversation is swirling around the classroom or you see a student's eyes light up with an "aha" moment.

I think of a 5th-grade student with severe reading issues. I learned he wanted to design a car engine that was self-sustaining, so I made an audio tape of the (adult) book, *Power Trip: From Oil Wells to Solar Cells—Our Ride to the Renewable Future* by Amanda Little, which he listened to as he read the book. At the end of each chapter, I asked him a few metacognitive questions. I wish you could have heard the electrical crackling of ideas that came from this young man.

Another student from the same class had made great strides in reading comprehension as he learned and applied Dr. Goodreader, shyly came up to my desk one day and said, "I know this probably sounds really weird, but sometimes I go so deep into Book World that I can actually see what is happening."

These are moments we treasure, and teaching with and for metacognition will give us many treasures to hoard in the secret places of our teaching hearts.

APPENDIX A
RECOMMENDED RESOURCES

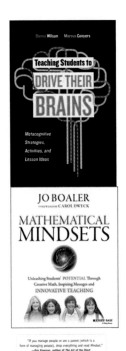

Teaching Students to Drive Their Brains by Donna Wilson and Marcus Conyers is a short read jam-packed with research and practical ideas for teaching metacognitively.

Jo Boaler's *Mathematical Mindsets: Unleashing students' potential through creative math, inspiring messages and innovative teaching* is my favorite educational book from 2016. It is an educational page-turner and I would recommend it for parents, teachers, and administrators who want their students to be "math people."

After reading Jo Boaler's book, I had to go back and pick up Carol Dweck's ground-breaking book, *Mindset: The New Psychology of Success*. Not only are fixed and growth mindset applied to the classroom, but in our relationships, businesses, and parenting. It was eye-opening for me in thinking about relationships.

Written by Peter Tarrant and Deborah Holt of the UK, *Metacognition in the Primary Classroom: A practical guide to helping children understand how they learn best* is that rare combination of scholarly, practical, and readable. They offer practical ideas for instituting a whole-school approach with metacognition and a plethora of easily implemented ideas for students 4 – 13 years old.

I just picked up this book in June and it is far and above my favorite educational read for 2017! *Creating Cultures of Thinking: The 8 forces we must master to truly transform our schools* by Ron Ritchhart challenges our thinking as educators in a way that is truly inspiring. Just the chapter on "Time" is worth the price of the book.

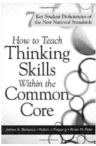

How to Teach Thinking Skills Within the Common Core by James A. Bellanca, Robin J. Fogarty, and Brian M. Pete addresses the whole idea of cognitive and metacognitive vocabulary with captivating lessons for elementary, middle, and high school. Do our students really know what it means to analyze? To understand? To synthesize? They will when you use this book.

APPENDIX B
METACOGNITIVE LANGUAGE

Applying	Demonstrating	Making changes	Retelling
Activating background knowledge	Describing	Making connections	Sequencing
Adding more detail	Determining	Modeling	Sequencing
Analyzing	Determining importance	Monitoring	Sense-making
Answering	Determining point of view	Noticing	Showing others
Asking	Developing	Organizing	Solving
Categorizing	Editing	Planning	Suggesting
Checking	Estimating	Problem-solving	Taking care
Choosing	Evaluating	Producing	Testing
Clarifying	Explaining	Proving	Thinking
Collaborating	Exploring	Reading/Writing	Thinking
Comparing	Finding relationships	Recalling	Thinking about relationships
Comprehending	Focusing on accuracy	Redrafting	Trying
Computing	Graphing	Reflecting	Trying out

Concentrating	Guessing	Remembering	Trying different ways
Considering	Identifying	Remembering other learning	Understanding
Contrasting	Improving	Revising	Using a plan
Creating	Inferring	Researching	Verifying
Deciding	Interpreting	Making changes	Visualizing
Decoding	Introducing	Making connections	Wondering

APPENDIX C
METACOGNITIVE JOURNEYS

I highly recommend thinking through metacognitive journeys that you have taken so that you can share them with your students. I have one from when I was a very unathletic cheerleader in 7th grade. I didn't think I could ever do a cartwheel, but I worked and worked with my family until I achieved ONE perfect cartwheel during the last basketball game of the season. I still remember the joy of that cartwheel. It should have had a sound track.

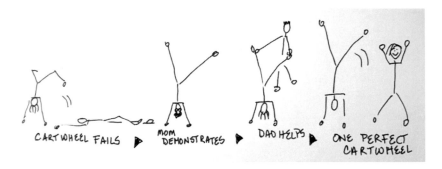

On a more serious note, I'm currently involved in another metacognitive journey:

I want to learn Bible Arcing, which is a way of linking the phrases in the Bible in 18 logical relationships, and I signed up for a course and doggedly plowed through it:

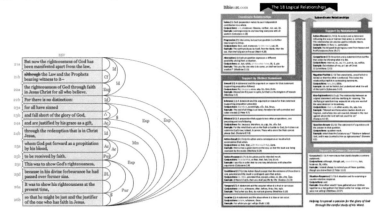

My feedback at the end of the course:

My response to the feedback that I received thanks to my recent learning about Fixed/Growth Mindsets:

I thought about how I could scaffold my learning and purchased a workbook on sentence diagramming because you need to make logical connections when you diagram:

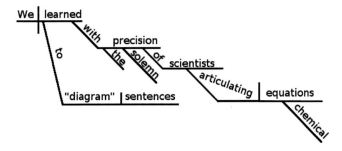

I took the most popular MOOC course, Learning How to Learn, and added a lot to my knowledge about learning something that is difficult for you. Some tips that really helped me are 1) the roll of exercise in thinking, 2) the fact that we switch from diffuse to focused thinking and back again and how switching can help learning, 3) the role of sleep in learning.

I followed that with a MOOC course on diagramming arguments which helped me straighten out some misconceptions I had about logical relationships.

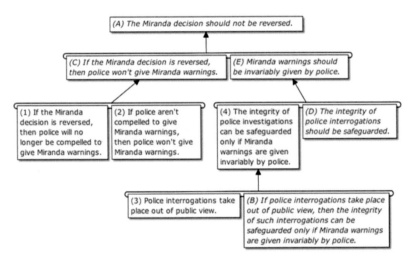

I am currently taking a course on Understanding Arguments which should add more to my background knowledge of logical relationships.

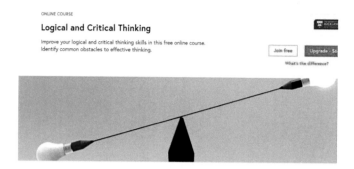

Logical and Critical Thinking

Improve your logical and critical thinking skills in this free online course.
Identify common obstacles to effective thinking.

Join free   Upgrade - $6

What's the difference?

And then I will retake the course on Bible Arcing. I have no amazing results to share YET, but I am confident I will in the future.

Share your journeys and refer to them when you teach.

FOOTNOTES

INTRODUCTION

[1] Stevens, S. (2012). *Dr. Goodreader*. Louisville, KY: Create Space.

CHAPTER 1

[1] Teal Center Staff. "Fact Sheet: Metacognitive Processes | Teaching Excellence in Adult Literacy (TEAL)." Fact Sheet: Metacognitive Processes | Teaching Excellence in Adult Literacy (TEAL). U.S. Department of Education, Feb. 2012. Web. 13 July 2016.

CHAPTER 2

[1] Wilson, D., & Conyers, M. (2016). *Teaching students to drive their brains: metacognitive strategies, activities, and lesson ideas.* Alexandria, VA: ASCD.

[2] Ibid

[3] Ibid

[4] Ibid

[5] Fisher, D., Frey, N., & Hattie, J. (2016). *Visible learning for literacy, grades K-12: implementing the practices that work best to accelerate student learning.* Thousand Oaks, CA: Corwin/A SAGE Company.

[6] On reading, Part 4: research on the comprehension strategies – a closer look. (2015, March 27). Retrieved July 18, 2017, from https://grantwiggins.wordpress.com/2015/03/26/on-reading-part-4-research-on-the-comprehension-strategies-a-closer-look/

[7] Wiggins, G. (2012, January 16). The research on transfer and some practical implications (Transfer, part 2). Retrieved July 18, 2017, from https://grantwiggins.wordpress.com/2012/01/16/the-research-on-transfer-and-some-practical-implications-transfer-part-2/

[8] How to Improve Metacognition in the Classroom. (n.d.). Retrieved July 18, 2017, from http://www.innerdrive.co.uk/improve-metacognition/

[9] Livingston, J. A. (1997). Metacognition: An Overview. Retrieved July 18, 2017, from http://gse.buffalo.edu/fas/shuell/cep564/metacog.htm

[10] PhD, M. P. (2015, April 07). Metacognition: Nurturing Self-Awareness in the Classroom. Retrieved July 18, 2017, from https://www.edutopia.org/blog/8-pathways-metacognition-in-classroom-marilyn-price-mitchell

[11] Pearson, Mildred M. Dr. and Harvey, Daniel P. II, "Cognitive Science: How Do Deep Approaches to Learning Promote Metacognitive Strategies to Enhance Integrated Learning?" (2013). Faculty Research and Creative Activity. Paper 31. http://thekeep.eiu.edu/eemedu_fac/31

[12] Ibid

[13] Wilson, D., & Conyers, M. (2016). *Teaching students to drive their brains: metacognitive strategies, activities, and lesson ideas.* Alexandria, VA: ASCD.

[14] Trilling, Bernie, and Maya Bialik. "The Role of Metacognition in Learning and Achievement." Four-Dimensional Education: The Competencies Learners Need to Succeed. By Charles Fadel. N.p.: n.p., n.d. N. pag. MindShift. 10 Aug. 2016. Web. 24 Aug. 2016.

[15] Hattie, J., & Anderman, E. M. (2013). *International guide to student achievement.* London: Routledge.

CHAPTER 4

[1] Wilson, D., & Conyers, M. (2016). *Teaching students to drive their brains: metacognitive strategies, activities, and lesson ideas.* Alexandria, VA: ASCD.

CHAPTER 6

[1] Boaler, Jo. (2016). *Mathematical Mindsets: unleashing students' potential through creative math, inspiring messages and innovative teaching.* San Francisco, CA: Jossey-Bass.

[2] Boaler, J. (2016). When You Believe In Yourself Your Brain Operates Differently. Retrieved July 19, 2017, from https://www.youcubed.org/think-it-up/believe-brain-operates-differently/

CHAPTER 7

[1] Teaching Metacognitive Skills. (2015, November 25). Retrieved July 20, 2017, from https://uwaterloo.ca/centre-for-teaching-excellence/teaching-resources/teaching-tips/metacognitive

[2] Tarrant, P., & Holt, D. (2016). *Metacognition in the primary classroom: a practical guide to helping children understand how they learn best.* London: Routledge, Taylor & Francis Group.

[3] Meta-cognition and self-regulation | Toolkit Strand. (2017, May 2). Retrieved July 20, 2017, from https://educationendowmentfoundation.org.uk/resources/teaching-learning-toolkit/meta-cognition-and-self-regulation/

[4] Wilhelm, J. D. (2003, March). Navigating Meaning: Using Think-Alouds to Help Readers Monitor Comprehension. Retrieved July 20, 2017, from https://www.nwp.org/cs/public/print/resource/495

[5] Overview of the Understanding Ideal. (n.d.). Retrieved July 20, 2017, from http://www.visiblethinkingpz.org/VisibleThinking_html_files/04_Thin kingIdeals/04c_UnderstandingIdeal.html

ABOUT THE AUTHOR

Susan Stevens has been in education since 1983 and has taught art PK – 12th grade; 5th grade; middle school ELA, math, and Bible; and even a little physical education, although that was NOT her finest hour. She has worked as Curriculum Coordinator at the pre-school, elementary, and middle school levels. She's also been Testing Coordinator. She has masters' degrees in Christian Education and Reading. Her experience spans public, private, and international schools. She currently works as an Educational Consultant in the areas of literacy and metacognition—her passions. She and her husband live across the street from the beach in St. Augustine, Florida and love living close to family.

Made in the USA
San Bernardino, CA
29 December 2018